Contents

The following practice exam paper is a printed representation of how this exam will appear when online. The structure of the questions, the knowledge required and the topics covered will be the same. However, in order to suit an online platform, the wording of the questions and the method of answering them may be different.

Terminology:

bar	semibreve	minim	crotchet	quaver	semiquaver
measure	whole note	half note	quarter note	8th note	16th note

Music Theory Practice Paper 2021 Grade 1 A

Exam duration: 1½ hours maximum

Total marks: /75

1 Rhythm

/15

1.1 Circle the correct time signature for each of these bars.

(3)

(a)

$\frac{2}{4}$ $\frac{4}{4}$ $\frac{3}{4}$

(b)

C $\frac{2}{4}$ $\frac{3}{4}$

(c)

$\frac{2}{4}$ $\frac{3}{4}$ **C**

1.2 Add the **one** missing bar-line to **each** of these five melodies.

(5)

(a)

(b)

(c)

(d)

(e)

1.3 Tick (✔) **one** box to answer each question.

(2)

(a) How many crotchets are there in a 𝅗𝅥. ?   2 ☐   3 ☐   4 ☐   5 ☐

(b) How many semiquavers are there in a semibreve?   4 ☐   8 ☐   12 ☐   16 ☐

1.4 Tick (✔) **one** box to show which bar is grouped correctly.

(1)

☐   ☐   ☐

1.5 Tick (✔) or cross (✘) **each** box to show whether the rests are correct **or** incorrect. (3)

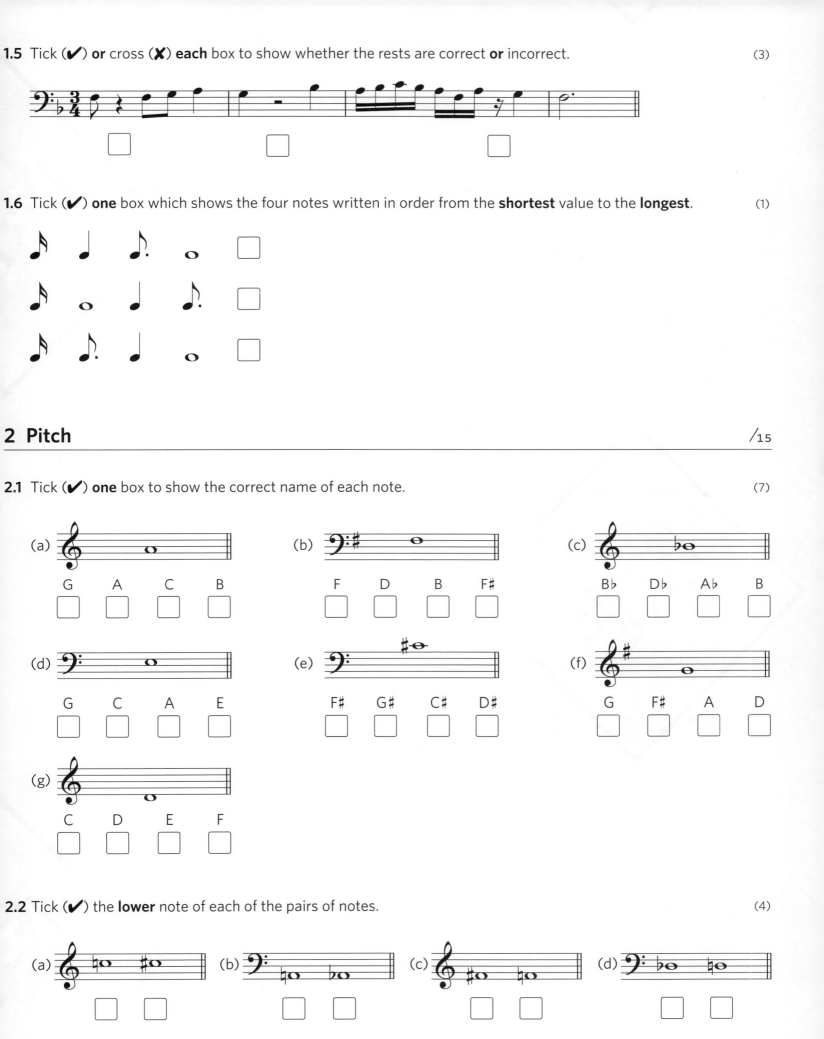

1.6 Tick (✔) **one** box which shows the four notes written in order from the **shortest** value to the **longest**. (1)

2 Pitch /15

2.1 Tick (✔) **one** box to show the correct name of each note. (7)

(a) G   A   C   B

(b) F   D   B   F♯

(c) B♭   D♭   A♭   B

(d) G   C   A   E

(e) F♯   G♯   C♯   D♯

(f) G   F♯   A   D

(g) C   D   E   F

2.2 Tick (✔) the **lower** note of each of the pairs of notes. (4)

(a)   (b)   (c)   (d)

2.3 Tick (✔) the correct clef needed to make each of these named notes. (4)

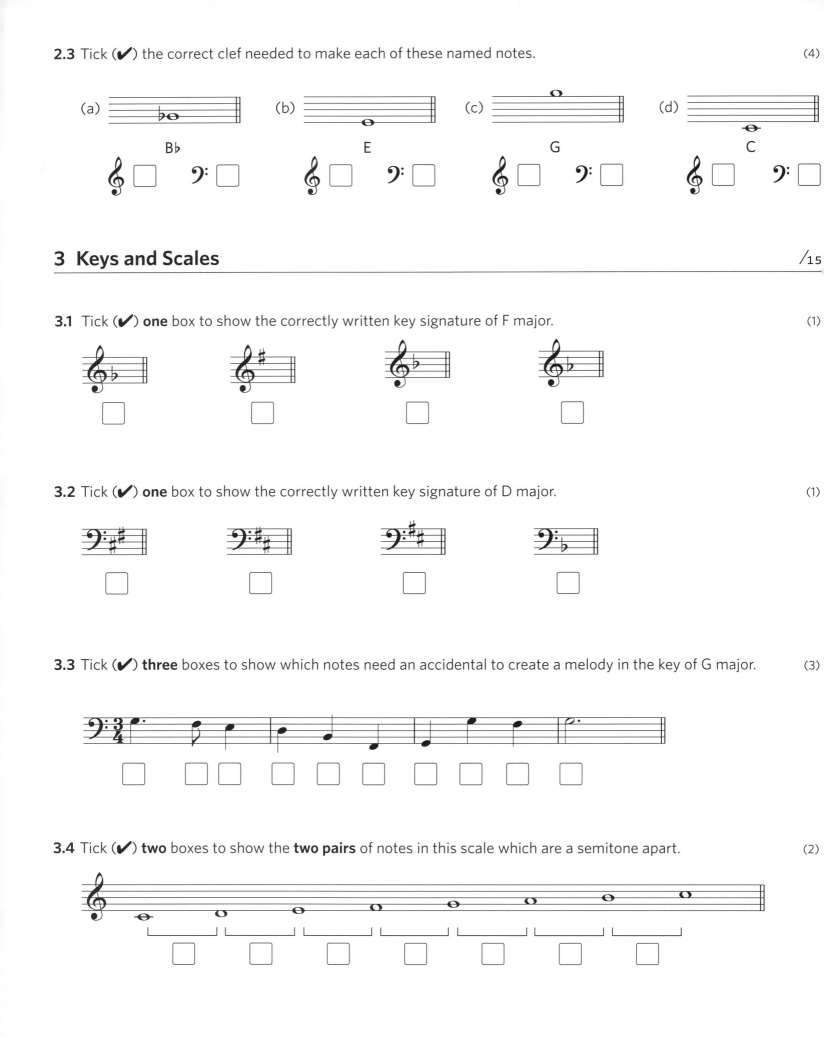

3 Keys and Scales /15

3.1 Tick (✔) **one** box to show the correctly written key signature of F major. (1)

3.2 Tick (✔) **one** box to show the correctly written key signature of D major. (1)

3.3 Tick (✔) **three** boxes to show which notes need an accidental to create a melody in the key of G major. (3)

3.4 Tick (✔) **two** boxes to show the **two pairs** of notes in this scale which are a semitone apart. (2)

3.5 Circle **TRUE** or **FALSE** for each statement. (4)

(a) There are no sharps or flats in the key signature of C major   **TRUE**   **FALSE**

(b) There are two sharps in the key signature of G major   **TRUE**   **FALSE**

(c) 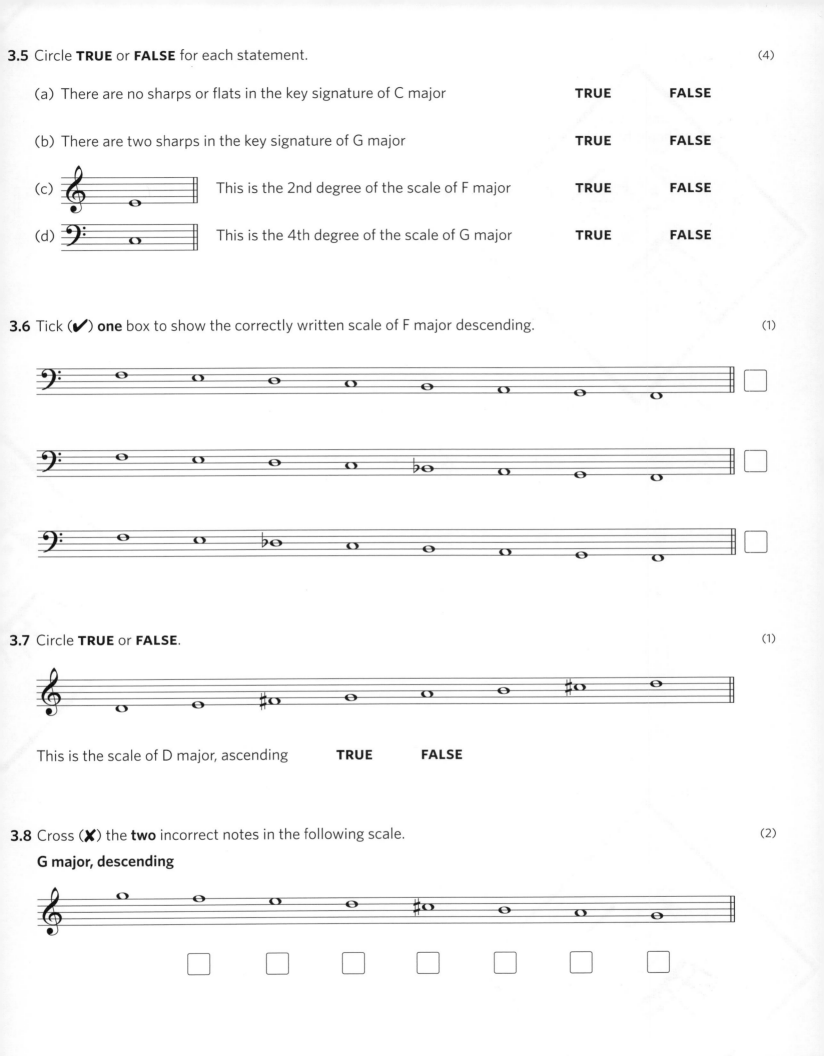 This is the 2nd degree of the scale of F major   **TRUE**   **FALSE**

(d) This is the 4th degree of the scale of G major   **TRUE**   **FALSE**

3.6 Tick (✔) **one** box to show the correctly written scale of F major descending. (1)

3.7 Circle **TRUE** or **FALSE**. (1)

This is the scale of D major, ascending   **TRUE**   **FALSE**

3.8 Cross (✗) the **two** incorrect notes in the following scale. (2)

G major, descending

4 Intervals

/10

4.1 For each example, write one note to form the named interval.
Your note should be **higher** than the given note. The key is G major.

(5)

5th

2nd

6th

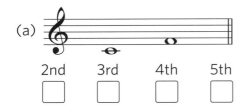

3rd

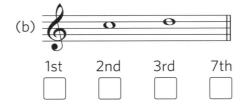

8th / 8ve

4.2 Tick (✔) **one** box to show the correct number of each interval. The key is C major.

(5)

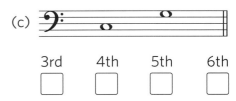

(a)

2nd	3rd	4th	5th
☐	☐	☐	☐

(b)

1st	2nd	3rd	7th
☐	☐	☐	☐

(c)

3rd	4th	5th	6th
☐	☐	☐	☐

(d)

3rd	4th	5th	6th
☐	☐	☐	☐

(e)

2nd	5th	7th	8th/8ve
☐	☐	☐	☐

5 Tonic Triads

/10

5.1 Circle **TRUE** or **FALSE** for each statement.

(3)

(a) This is the tonic triad of C major   **TRUE**   **FALSE**

(b) This is the tonic triad of F major   **TRUE**   **FALSE**

(c) This is the tonic triad of D major   **TRUE**   **FALSE**

5.2 Add **one** missing note to complete each triad, with the tonic as the lowest note. (3)
Use accidentals if necessary.

(a) [bass clef, G major triad]

G major

(b) [treble clef, F major triad]

F major

(c) [bass clef, C major triad]

C major

5.3 Circle the correct key for each tonic triad. (4)

(a) [treble clef triad]

| F major | D major | G major | C major |

(b) [treble clef triad]

| C major | G major | F major | D major |

(c) [bass clef triad]

| D major | F major | G major | C major |

(d) [bass clef triad]

| D major | F major | C major | G major |

6 Terms and Signs   /5

Tick (✔) **one** box for each term/sign. (5)

Allegro means:

at a moderate speed	☐
slow	☐
quick	☐
fairly quick	☐

da capo means:

repeat from the beginning	☐
in a singing style	☐
up to the end	☐
in time	☐

mf means:

loud	☐
very quiet	☐
moderately quiet	☐
moderately loud	☐

⌢ means:

legato: smoothly	☐
staccato: detached	☐
pause on the note or rest	☐
accent the note	☐

accelerando means:

gradually getting louder	☐
gradually getting quieter	☐
gradually getting slower	☐
gradually getting quicker	☐

Look at this melody and then answer the questions that follow.

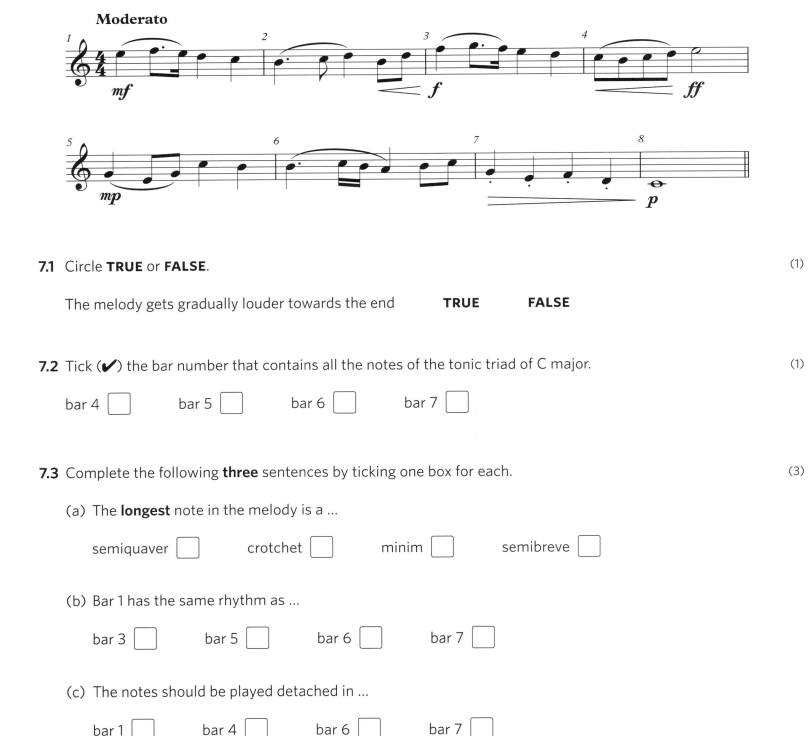

7.1 Circle **TRUE** or **FALSE**. (1)

The melody gets gradually louder towards the end   **TRUE**   **FALSE**

7.2 Tick (✔) the bar number that contains all the notes of the tonic triad of C major. (1)

bar 4 ☐   bar 5 ☐   bar 6 ☐   bar 7 ☐

7.3 Complete the following **three** sentences by ticking one box for each. (3)

(a) The **longest** note in the melody is a …

semiquaver ☐   crotchet ☐   minim ☐   semibreve ☐

(b) Bar 1 has the same rhythm as …

bar 3 ☐   bar 5 ☐   bar 6 ☐   bar 7 ☐

(c) The notes should be played detached in …

bar 1 ☐   bar 4 ☐   bar 6 ☐   bar 7 ☐

Music Theory Practice Paper 2021 Grade 1 B

Exam duration: 1½ hours maximum

Total marks: ___ /75

1 Rhythm /15

1.1 Circle the correct time signature for each of these bars. (3)

(a)

$\frac{3}{4}$ $\frac{4}{4}$ $\frac{2}{4}$

(b)

$\frac{2}{4}$ **C** $\frac{3}{4}$

(c)

$\frac{4}{4}$ $\frac{3}{4}$ $\frac{2}{4}$

1.2 Add the **one** missing bar-line to **each** of these five melodies. (5)

(a)

(b)

(c)

(d)

(e)

1.3 Tick (✔) **one** box to answer each question. (2)

(a) How many semiquavers are there in a ?   3 ☐   4 ☐   5 ☐   6 ☐

(b) How many quavers are there in a minim?   2 ☐   4 ☐   8 ☐   12 ☐

1.4 Tick (✔) **one** box to show which bar is grouped correctly. (1)

☐   ☐   ☐

Turn the page

1.5 Tick (✔) or cross (✘) **each** box to show whether the rests are correct **or** incorrect. (3)

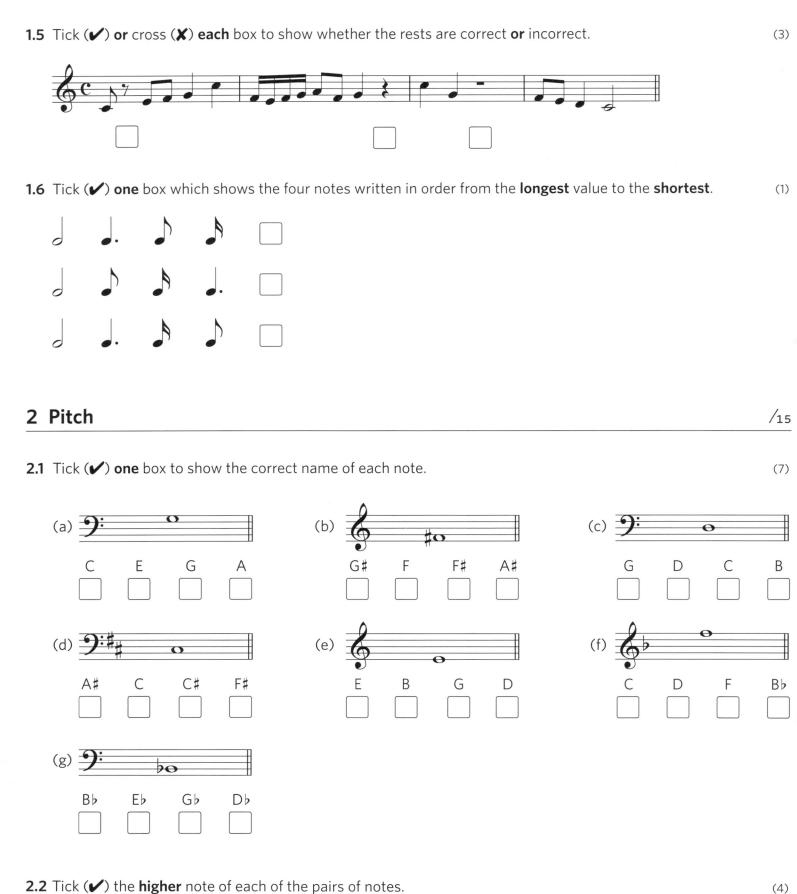

1.6 Tick (✔) **one** box which shows the four notes written in order from the **longest** value to the **shortest**. (1)

2 Pitch

2.1 Tick (✔) **one** box to show the correct name of each note. (7)

(a)

| C | E | G | A |
| □ | □ | □ | □ |

(b)

| G♯ | F | F♯ | A♯ |
| □ | □ | □ | □ |

(c)

| G | D | C | B |
| □ | □ | □ | □ |

(d)

| A♯ | C | C♯ | F♯ |
| □ | □ | □ | □ |

(e)

| E | B | G | D |
| □ | □ | □ | □ |

(f)

| C | D | F | B♭ |
| □ | □ | □ | □ |

(g)

| B♭ | E♭ | G♭ | D♭ |
| □ | □ | □ | □ |

2.2 Tick (✔) the **higher** note of each of the pairs of notes. (4)

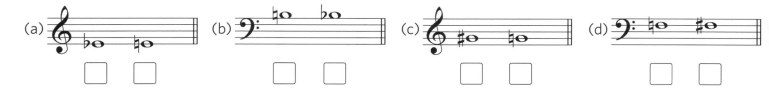

2.3 Tick (✔) the correct clef needed to make each of these named notes. (4)

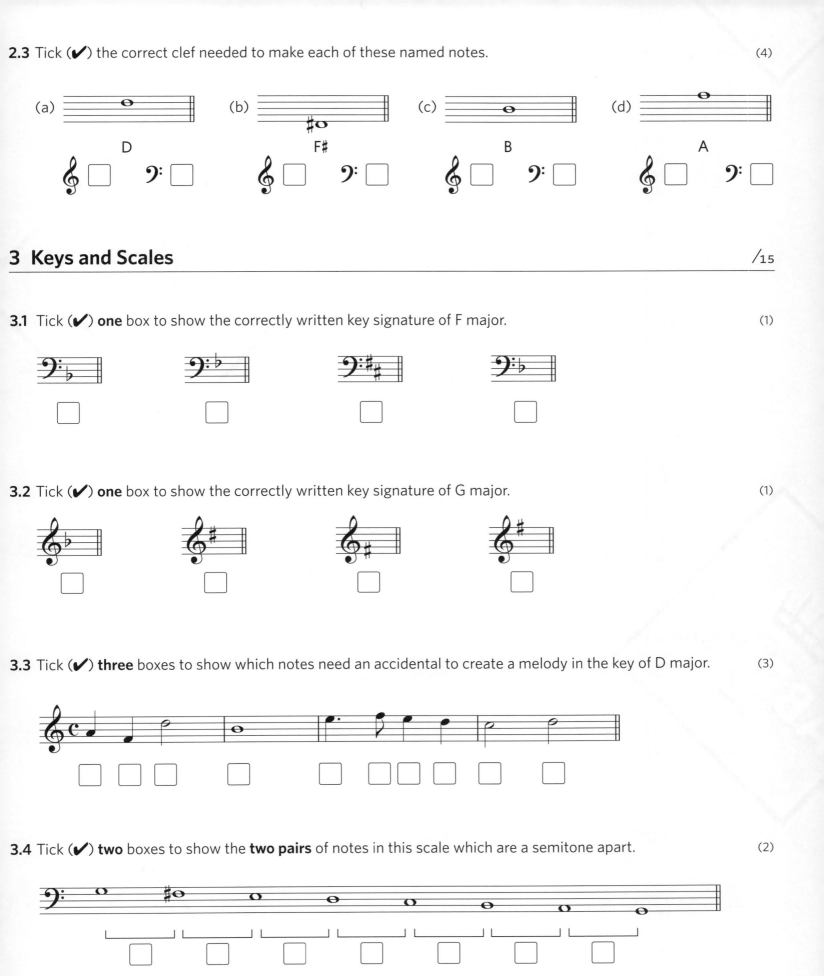

3 Keys and Scales /15

3.1 Tick (✔) **one** box to show the correctly written key signature of F major. (1)

3.2 Tick (✔) **one** box to show the correctly written key signature of G major. (1)

3.3 Tick (✔) **three** boxes to show which notes need an accidental to create a melody in the key of D major. (3)

3.4 Tick (✔) **two** boxes to show the **two pairs** of notes in this scale which are a semitone apart. (2)

3.5 Circle **TRUE** or **FALSE** for each statement.   (4)

(a) There are two sharps in the key signature of D major   **TRUE**   **FALSE**

(b) There is one sharp in the key signature of C major   **TRUE**   **FALSE**

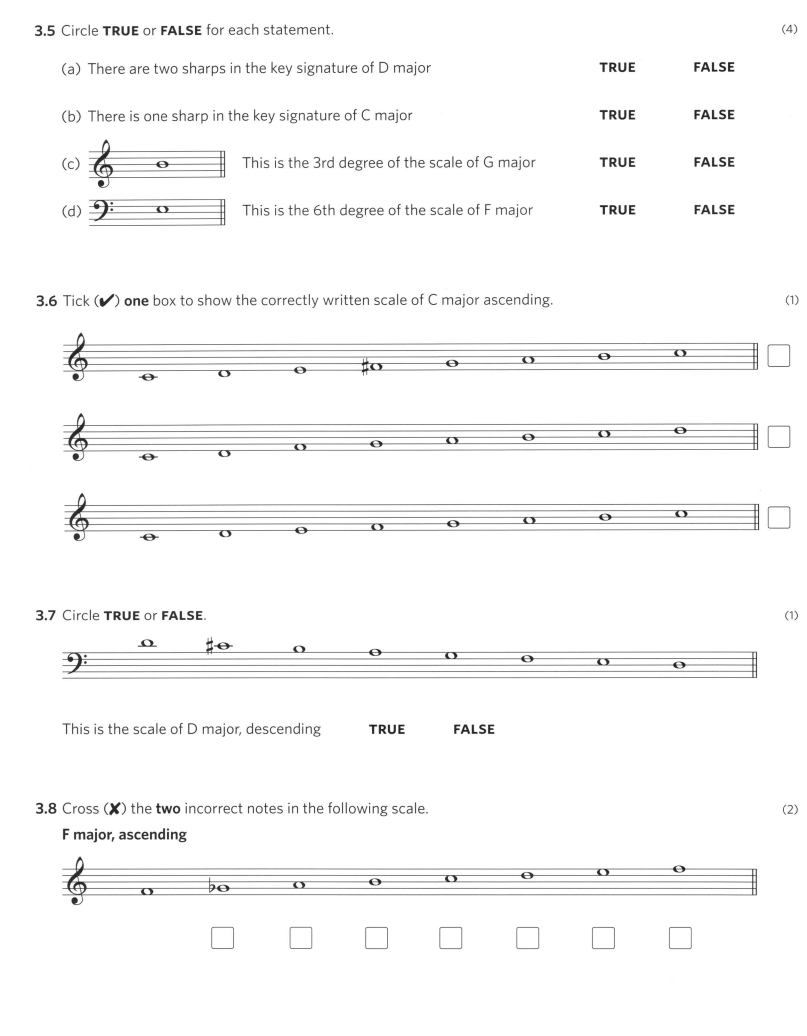

(c) This is the 3rd degree of the scale of G major   **TRUE**   **FALSE**

(d) This is the 6th degree of the scale of F major   **TRUE**   **FALSE**

3.6 Tick (✔) **one** box to show the correctly written scale of C major ascending.   (1)

3.7 Circle **TRUE** or **FALSE**.   (1)

This is the scale of D major, descending   **TRUE**   **FALSE**

3.8 Cross (✗) the **two** incorrect notes in the following scale.   (2)

F major, ascending

4 Intervals /10

4.1 For each example, write one note to form the named interval.
Your note should be **higher** than the given note. The key is F major.   (5)

(a)

8th / 8ve

(b)

2nd

(c)

3rd

(d)

7th

(e)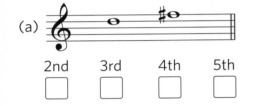

5th

4.2 Tick (✔) **one** box to show the correct number of each interval. The key is D major.   (5)

(a)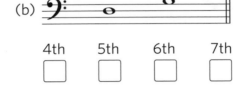

| 2nd | 3rd | 4th | 5th |
| ☐ | ☐ | ☐ | ☐ |

(b)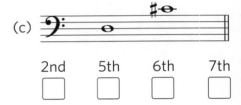

| 4th | 5th | 6th | 7th |
| ☐ | ☐ | ☐ | ☐ |

(c)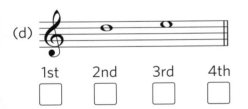

| 2nd | 5th | 6th | 7th |
| ☐ | ☐ | ☐ | ☐ |

(d)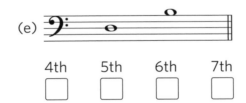

| 1st | 2nd | 3rd | 4th |
| ☐ | ☐ | ☐ | ☐ |

(e)

| 4th | 5th | 6th | 7th |
| ☐ | ☐ | ☐ | ☐ |

5 Tonic Triads /10

5.1 Circle **TRUE** or **FALSE** for each statement.   (3)

(a)   This is the tonic triad of C major   **TRUE**   **FALSE**

(b)   This is the tonic triad of G major   **TRUE**   **FALSE**

(c)   This is the tonic triad of F major   **TRUE**   **FALSE**

5.2 Add **one** missing note to complete each triad, with the tonic as the lowest note. (3)
Use accidentals if necessary.

(a) [bass clef with triad]
C major

(b) [treble clef with ♯ triad]
D major

(c) [treble clef with triad]
F major

5.3 Circle the correct key for each tonic triad. (4)

(a) [bass clef triad]   C major   F major   G major   D major

(b) [bass clef ♯ triad]   G major   F major   C major   D major

(c) [treble clef triad]   D major   G major   F major   C major

(d) [treble clef triad]   G major   C major   D major   F major

6 Terms and Signs

/5

Tick (✔) **one** box for each term/sign. (5)

Moderato means:

moderately quiet ☐

at a moderate pace ☐

gradually getting slower ☐

moderately loud ☐

a tempo means:

in time ☐

up to the end ☐

slow ☐

gradually getting quicker ☐

pp means:

loud ☐

quiet ☐

very loud ☐

very quiet ☐

♩ = 60 means:

60 crotchet notes ☐

60 crotchets in one beat ☐

60 crotchet beats in a minute ☐

60 crotchets in the melody ☐

[slur/tie symbol] means:

slur: perform smoothly ☐

tie: detached ☐

tie: hold for the value of both notes ☐

pause on the notes ☐

Look at this melody and then answer the questions that follow.

7.1 Circle **TRUE** or **FALSE**.   (1)

The melody gets gradually louder in bar 3   **TRUE**   **FALSE**

7.2 Tick (✔) one box to show how many times the rhythm ♩. ♪ ♩ occurs.   (1)

1 ☐   2 ☐   3 ☐   4 ☐

7.3 Complete the following **three** sentences by ticking one box for each.   (3)

(a) The **longest** note in the melody is a …

dotted minim ☐   semibreve ☐   dotted crotchet ☐   minim ☐

(b) The lowest note in the melody is …

D ☐   C♯ ☐   E ☐   A ☐

(c) All the notes should be played smoothly in …

bar 1 ☐   bar 2 ☐   bar 3 ☐   bar 4 ☐

Music Theory Practice Paper 2021 Grade 1 C

Exam duration: 1½ hours maximum

1 Rhythm /15

1.1 Circle the correct time signature for each of these bars. (3)

1.2 Add the **one** missing bar-line to **each** of these five melodies. (5)

1.3 Tick (✔) **one** box to answer each question. (2)

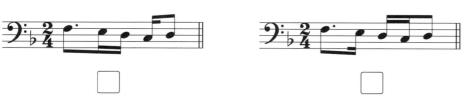

1.4 Tick (✔) **one** box to show which bar is grouped correctly. (1)

1.5 Tick (✔) or cross (✘) **each** box to show whether the rests are correct **or** incorrect. (3)

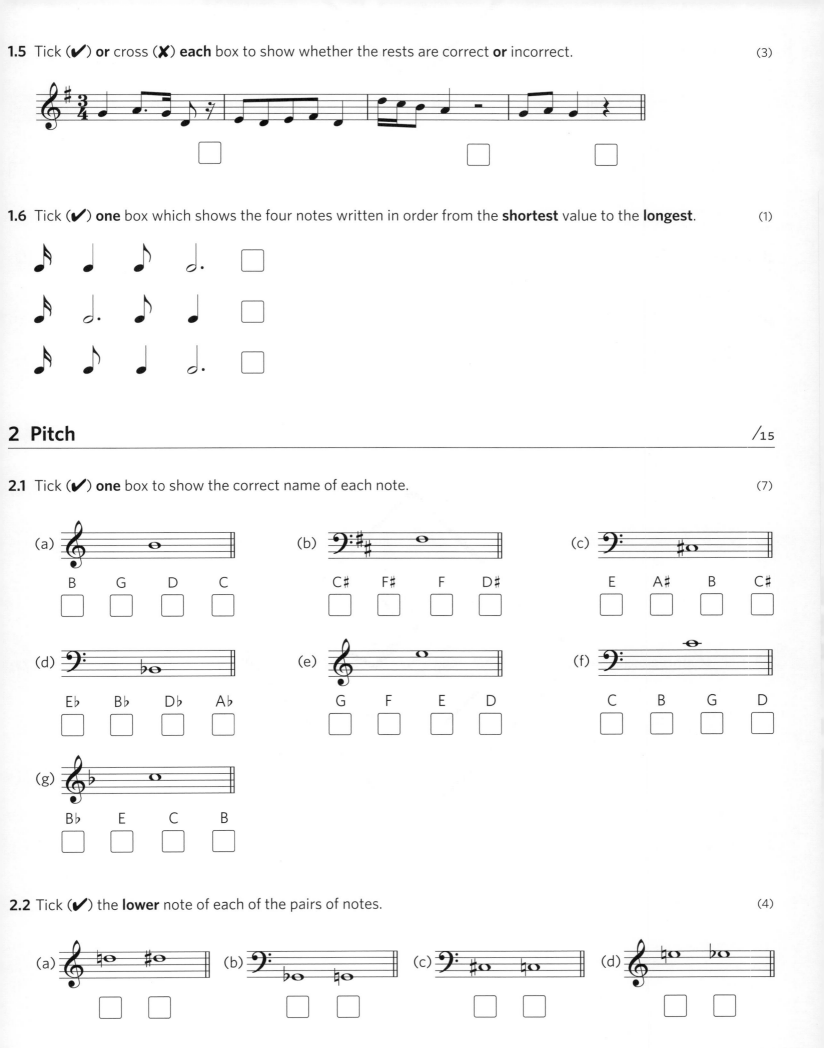

1.6 Tick (✔) **one** box which shows the four notes written in order from the **shortest** value to the **longest**. (1)

2 Pitch /15

2.1 Tick (✔) **one** box to show the correct name of each note. (7)

(a) B G D C

(b) C# F# F D#

(c) E A# B C#

(d) Eb Bb Db Ab

(e) G F E D

(f) C B G D

(g) Bb E C B

2.2 Tick (✔) the **lower** note of each of the pairs of notes. (4)

(a) (b) (c) (d)

2.3 Tick (✔) the correct clef needed to make each of these named notes. (4)

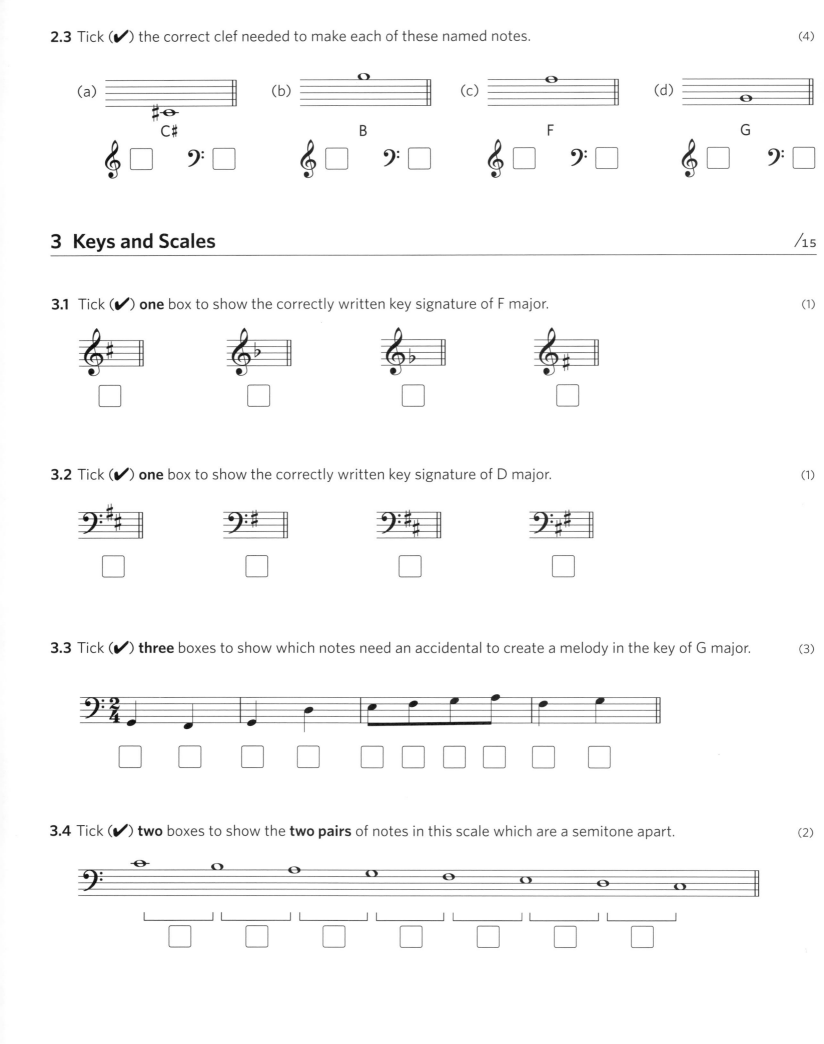

3 Keys and Scales /15

3.1 Tick (✔) **one** box to show the correctly written key signature of F major. (1)

3.2 Tick (✔) **one** box to show the correctly written key signature of D major. (1)

3.3 Tick (✔) **three** boxes to show which notes need an accidental to create a melody in the key of G major. (3)

3.4 Tick (✔) **two** boxes to show the **two pairs** of notes in this scale which are a semitone apart. (2)

3.5 Circle **TRUE** or **FALSE** for each statement. (4)

(a) There is one flat in the key signature of G major   **TRUE**   **FALSE**

(b) There are no sharps or flats in the key signature of C major   **TRUE**   **FALSE**

(c) 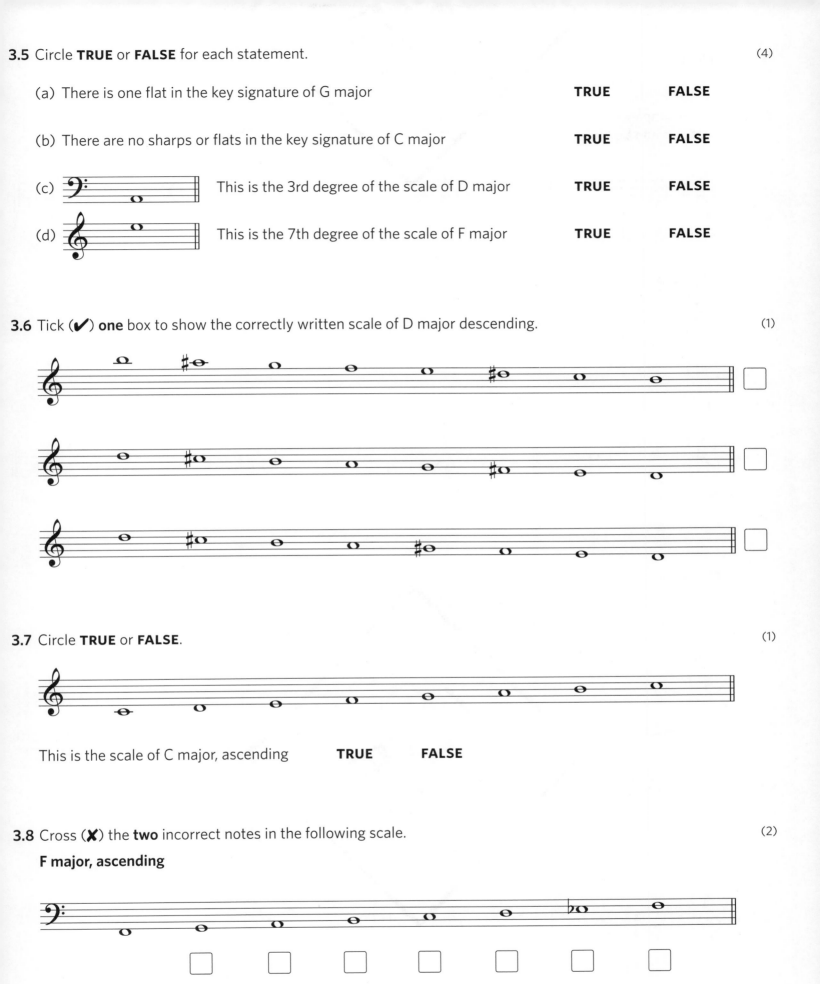 This is the 3rd degree of the scale of D major   **TRUE**   **FALSE**

(d) This is the 7th degree of the scale of F major   **TRUE**   **FALSE**

3.6 Tick (✔) **one** box to show the correctly written scale of D major descending. (1)

3.7 Circle **TRUE** or **FALSE**. (1)

This is the scale of C major, ascending   **TRUE**   **FALSE**

3.8 Cross (✘) the **two** incorrect notes in the following scale. (2)

F major, ascending

4 Intervals

4.1 For each example, write one note to form the named interval. (5)
Your note should be **higher** than the given note. The key is G major.

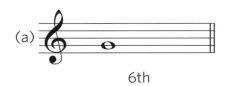

(a)

6th

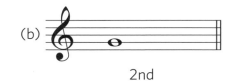

(b)

2nd

(c)

4th

(d)

3rd

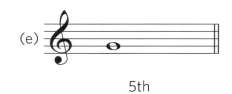

(e)

5th

4.2 Tick (✔) **one** box to show the correct number of each interval. The key is F major. (5)

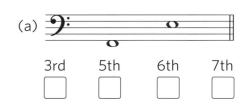

(a)

3rd	5th	6th	7th
☐	☐	☐	☐

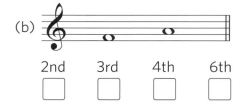

(b)

2nd	3rd	4th	6th
☐	☐	☐	☐

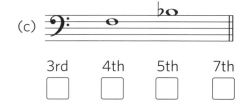

(c)

3rd	4th	5th	7th
☐	☐	☐	☐

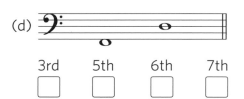

(d)

3rd	5th	6th	7th
☐	☐	☐	☐

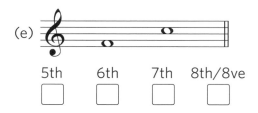

(e)

5th	6th	7th	8th/8ve
☐	☐	☐	☐

5 Tonic Triads

5.1 Circle **TRUE** or **FALSE** for each statement. (3)

(a)   This is the tonic triad of G major   **TRUE**   **FALSE**

(b)   This is the tonic triad of F major   **TRUE**   **FALSE**

(c)   This is the tonic triad of C major   **TRUE**   **FALSE**

5.2 Add **one** missing note to complete each triad, with the tonic as the lowest note. (3)
Use accidentals if necessary.

(a) D major

(b) F major

(c) C major

5.3 Circle the correct key for each tonic triad. (4)

(a) F major   C major   D major   G major

(b) C major   D major   G major   F major

(c) D major   G major   C major   F major

(d) D major   G major   F major   C major

6 Terms and Signs /5

Tick (✔) **one** box for each term/sign. (5)

Andante means:

quick ☐

in a singing style ☐

gradually getting quicker ☐

at a medium speed ☐

mf means:

moderately loud ☐

loud ☐

moderately quiet ☐

at a moderate speed ☐

legato means:

slow ☐

detached ☐

smoothly ☐

gradually getting slower ☐

⟍ means:

gradually getting louder ☐

accent the note ☐

quiet ☐

gradually getting quieter ☐

⌢ means:

accent the note ☐

staccato: detached ☐

pause on the note or rest ☐

perform the notes smoothly ☐

Look at this melody and then answer the questions that follow.

7.1 Circle **TRUE** or **FALSE**. (1)

The melody gets gradually quicker towards the end   **TRUE**   **FALSE**

7.2 Tick (✔) one box to show how many times the rhythm occurs. (1)

3 ☐   4 ☐   6 ☐   7 ☐

7.3 Complete the following **three** sentences by ticking one box for each. (3)

    (a) The **longest** rest in the melody is a …

        quaver rest ☐   semibreve rest ☐   minim rest ☐   crotchet rest ☐

    (b) The highest note in the melody is …

        F ☐   E ☐   G ☐   C ☐

    (c) All the notes should be played smoothly in …

        bar 1 ☐   bar 4 ☐   bar 6 ☐   bar 7 ☐

Music Theory Practice Paper 2021 Grade 1 D

Exam duration: 1½ hours maximum

Total marks: /75

1 Rhythm

/15

1.1 Circle the correct time signature for each of these bars.

(3)

(a)

$\frac{2}{4}$ **c** $\frac{3}{4}$

(b)

$\frac{4}{4}$ $\frac{3}{4}$ $\frac{2}{4}$

(c)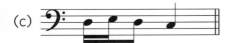

c $\frac{2}{4}$ $\frac{3}{4}$

1.2 Add the **one** missing bar-line to **each** of these five melodies.

(5)

(a)

(b)

(c)

(d)

(e)

1.3 Tick (✔) **one** box to answer each question.

(2)

(a) How many semiquavers are there in a ♩ ?   4 ☐   6 ☐   8 ☐   12 ☐

(b) How many quavers are there in a dotted crotchet?   2 ☐   3 ☐   5 ☐   6 ☐

1.4 Tick (✔) **one** box to show which bar is grouped correctly.

(1)

☐

☐

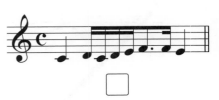

☐

Turn the page

1.5 Tick (✔) or cross (✘) **each** box to show whether the rests are correct **or** incorrect. (3)

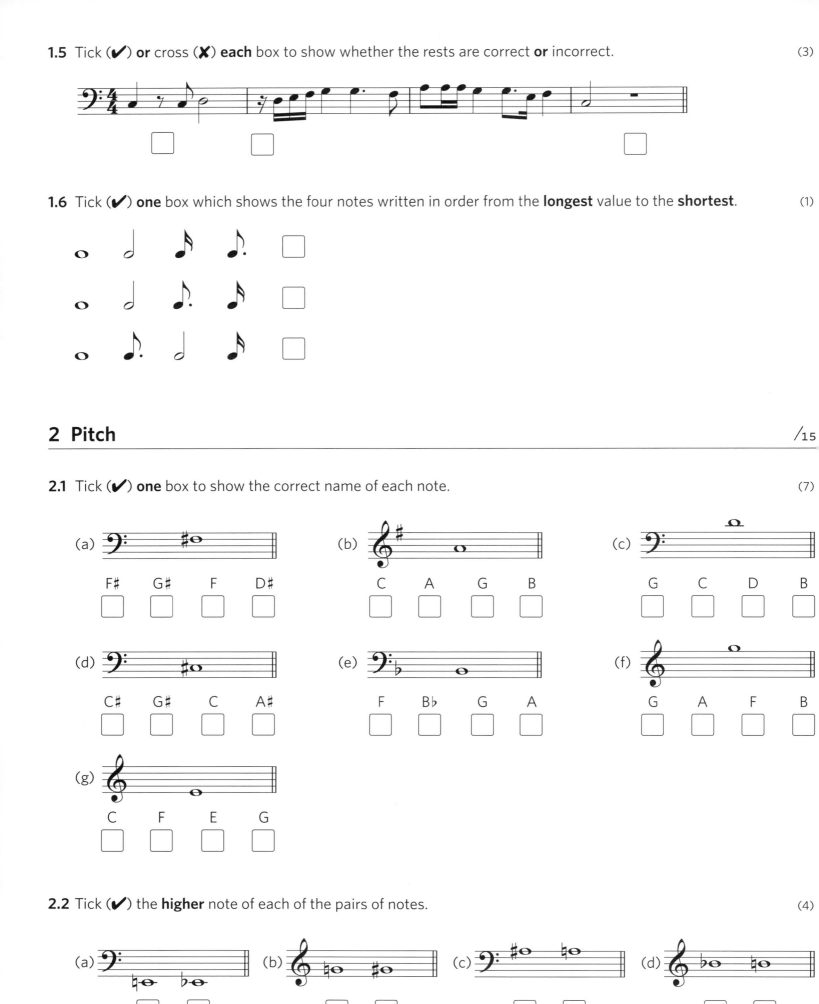

1.6 Tick (✔) **one** box which shows the four notes written in order from the **longest** value to the **shortest**. (1)

2 Pitch /15

2.1 Tick (✔) **one** box to show the correct name of each note. (7)

(a) F♯ G♯ F D♯

(b) C A G B

(c) G C D B

(d) C♯ G♯ C A♯

(e) F B♭ G A

(f) G A F B

(g) C F E G

2.2 Tick (✔) the **higher** note of each of the pairs of notes. (4)

(a) (b) (c) (d)

2.3 Tick (✔) the correct clef needed to make each of these named notes. (4)

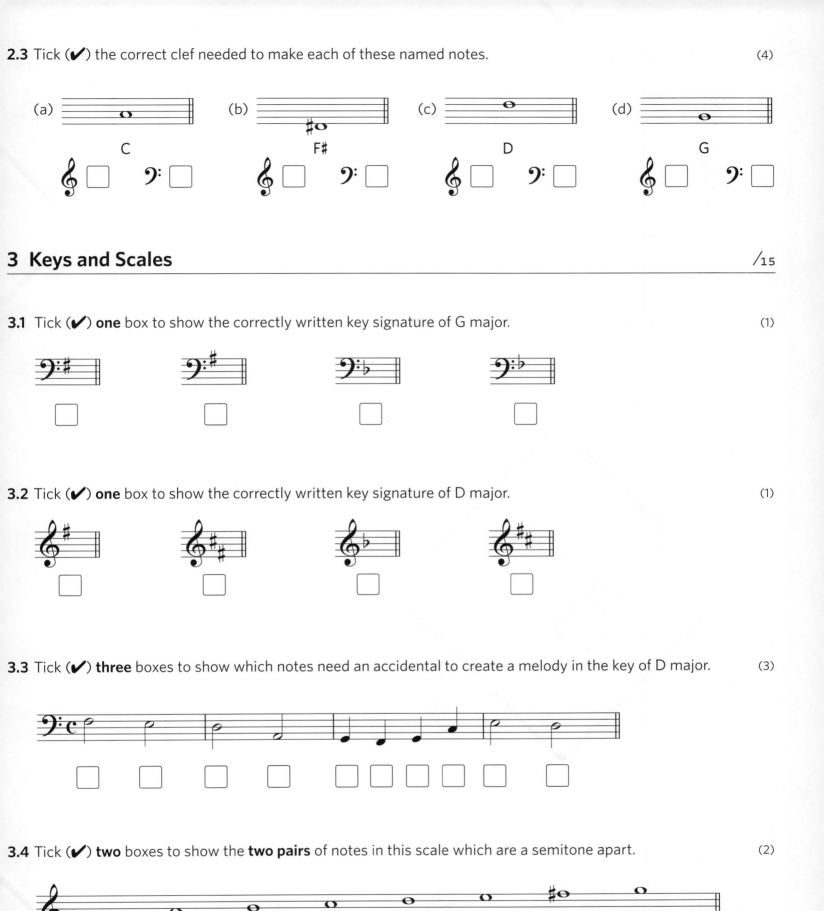

3 Keys and Scales /15

3.1 Tick (✔) **one** box to show the correctly written key signature of G major. (1)

3.2 Tick (✔) **one** box to show the correctly written key signature of D major. (1)

3.3 Tick (✔) **three** boxes to show which notes need an accidental to create a melody in the key of D major. (3)

3.4 Tick (✔) **two** boxes to show the **two pairs** of notes in this scale which are a semitone apart. (2)

3.5 Circle **TRUE** or **FALSE** for each statement. (4)

(a) There is one flat in the key signature of F major TRUE FALSE

(b) There are no sharps or flats in the key signature of C major TRUE FALSE

(c) 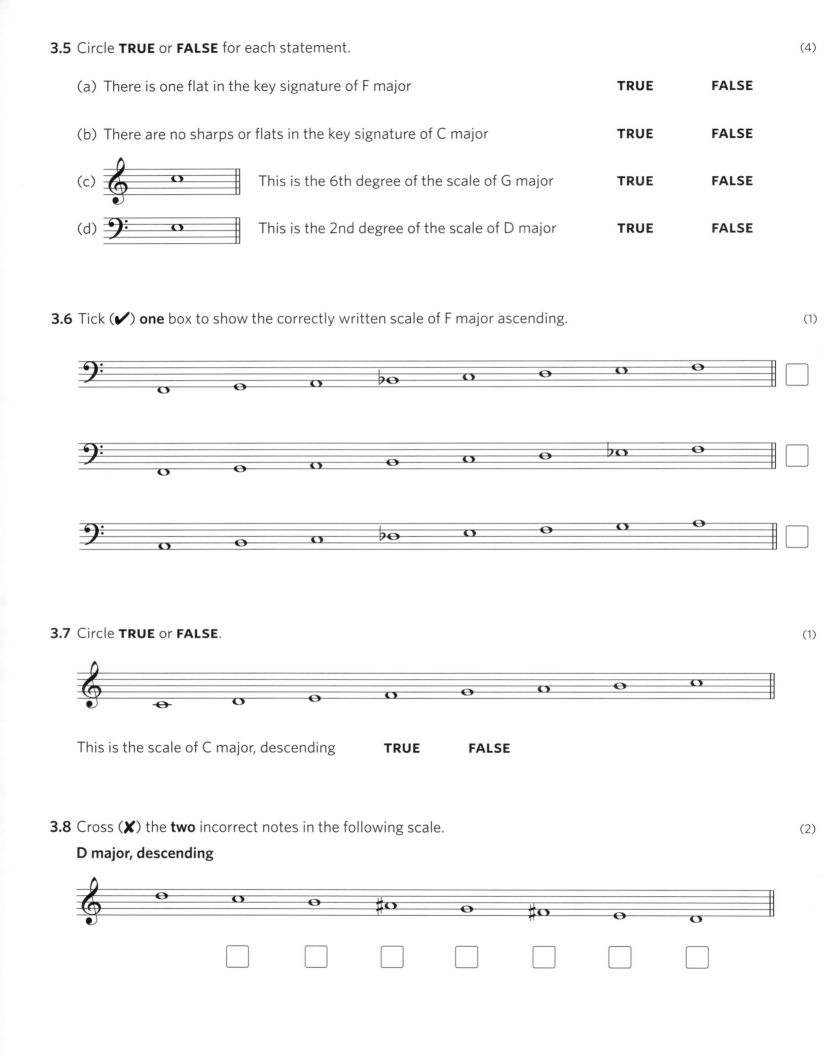 This is the 6th degree of the scale of G major TRUE FALSE

(d) This is the 2nd degree of the scale of D major TRUE FALSE

3.6 Tick (✔) **one** box to show the correctly written scale of F major ascending. (1)

3.7 Circle **TRUE** or **FALSE**. (1)

This is the scale of C major, descending TRUE FALSE

3.8 Cross (✗) the **two** incorrect notes in the following scale. (2)

D major, descending

4 Intervals

/10

4.1 For each example, write one note to form the named interval.
Your note should be **higher** than the given note. The key is C major.

(5)

(a)

4th

(b)

3rd

(c)

7th

(d)

6th

(e)

5th

4.2 Tick (✔) **one** box to show the correct number of each interval. The key is G major.

(5)

(a)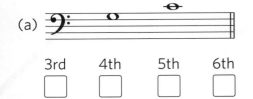

3rd	4th	5th	6th
☐	☐	☐	☐

(b)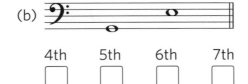

4th	5th	6th	7th
☐	☐	☐	☐

(c)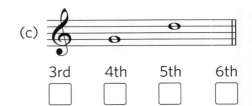

3rd	4th	5th	6th
☐	☐	☐	☐

(d)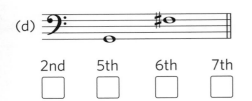

2nd	5th	6th	7th
☐	☐	☐	☐

(e)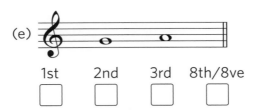

1st	2nd	3rd	8th/8ve
☐	☐	☐	☐

5 Tonic Triads

/10

5.1 Circle **TRUE** or **FALSE** for each statement.

(3)

(a)    This is the tonic triad of D major   **TRUE**   **FALSE**

(b) This is the tonic triad of F major   **TRUE**   **FALSE**

(c) This is the tonic triad of C major   **TRUE**   **FALSE**

5.2 Add **one** missing note to complete each triad, with the tonic as the lowest note. (3)
Use accidentals if necessary.

(a)

G major

(b)

C major

(c)

F major

5.3 Circle the correct key for each tonic triad. (4)

(a)   D major   G major   F major   C major

(b)   F major   C major   D major   G major

(c)   D major   F major   C major   G major

(d)   F major   C major   G major   D major

6 Terms and Signs /5

Tick (✔) **one** box for each term/sign. (5)

♩ = 68 means:

68 crotchet beats	☐
68 crotchet beats in a minute	☐
68 crotchet beats in a bar	☐
68 crotchets in one beat	☐

⌒ means:

slur: perform smoothly	☐
tie: detached	☐
tie: hold for the value of both notes	☐
slur: detached	☐

pp means:

moderately quiet	☐
very loud	☐
quiet	☐
very quiet	☐

fine means:

the end	☐
in time	☐
smoothly	☐
repeat from the beginning	☐

cantabile means:

slow	☐
gradually getting quieter	☐
at a medium speed	☐
in a singing style	☐